Mindfuln‹

MW01288675

How to Drastically Transform All Areas of Your Life & Health with Powerful Mindfulness Techniques (That Anyone Can Master)

By Marta Tuchowska

www.holisticwellnessproject.com

www.amazon.com/author/mtuchowska

Contents

Introduction

Let me start with a bold statement - if you are a seeker type of person, you have probably read different self-help, personal development, and spirituality books and still feel like you have a lot of self-improvement work to do. Maybe you feel stuck or overwhelmed with all of the information you've gathered. The book you are reading now aims to make your journey simple, doable, and fun.

It's a fluff-free, practical guide designed to help you make friends with mindfulness and make it your lifestyle so that you can get honest with yourself and enjoy the process of your transformation. There will be no rainbows or unicorns because the approach I want to take is to understand and accept our reality first so that we know where we are. As soon as we know where we are, we can take the necessary action to change our direction if needed.

So while I can't promise the world, and I am definitely not a spiritual guru and do not want to become one, I am really excited for this mindfulness journey we are just about to embark on together. As always, I write in a simple, conversational style. I want you to feel as if you are talking to a friend over a nice cup of coffee. In this case- a mindfulness cup of coffee that will help you awaken your mind and soul to help you take necessary actions aligned with your true self. This is how you will be able to start transforming your life the way you want. Through the following pages of this book, you will first learn what mindfulness really is and how it translates to awareness, self-love, and self-honesty. You will then learn how to apply mindfulness in different life situations so that you can enjoy better quality of life.

Sound good?

Without further ado, let's get down to it!

Chapter 1 What Mindfulness Is Not

There are many books on mindfulness and many definitions of what mindfulness is, what it's not, and how you can achieve this mindful lifestyle quickly in certain amount of steps if you attend the guru's X seminar or buy his expensive certification program. Don't get me wrong, I have nothing against retreats or programs. There is always something to learn. However, the approach I take on in this book is a really simple, common sense approach. The definitions and explanations I present are based on my own experiences with mindfulness and how I use it to improve my health, life, career, and relationships, and how you can use it too. This book is not about me, it's about you.

Simple Rules of Mindfulness

Here's what I believe mindfulness is all about:

-It's a state that helps you notice things as they are - not too negative and not too positive. You see and realize things exactly as they are, without any judgment or unnecessary emotions that can result in anxious states.

-Mindfulness helps us be more aware. Awareness takes some time to master, and even the most spiritual gurus never master it fully. When we are aware, we can dive deep and learn how to solve our problems in a holistic way. Now, when I say holistic, I'm not referring to herbs, homeopathy, or essential oils (don't get me wrong, I am really into all this stuff, but there is much more to the word "holistic"). By saying "holistic", I mean taking a "whole-istic" approach and getting to the root of the problem. This may mean getting a bit uncomfortable and asking yourself questions that make you leave your comfort zone. For example, a person may tend to overspend or have a few too many drinks here and there. It may take some time to dive deep and understand the root of the problem - maybe this person is trying to escape sadness and loneliness? Maybe they need instant relaxation, which is what shopping and drinking provides to them? By becoming more aware of the situation, they can actually take action to do something about it. Mind that I have nothing against shopping, buying nice things, or enjoying an occasional drink with a good friend. It's when we are not aware of what we are really doing that our habits may turn problematic. So this is where mindfulness can help develop self-awareness

-Mindfulness is like a muscle. If you feel like you are not mindful, it's simply because you need to spend more time growing and stretching this muscle. This is something that many people overlook, and I have been guilty of this as well. After all, there are so many things to focus on in this day and age! We want to be happier, slimmer, more successful and what not. But... the good news is that when we try to practice mindfulness, achieving success, health, and whatever it is we have on our goal list becomes a lot easier. Yes, I know it all sounds a bit hippie dippie combined with an over marketed line, "Just be mindful and love yourself, and you will achieve health, wealth, and happiness in 7 days or less. Click here to learn how, for only $697. Can be paid in 7 easy installments!"

We get exposed to lines like, "Raise your awareness, raise your consciousness, even raise your pH and it will all be fine." But really, it takes some work, commitment, and honest moments of realization of what you actually can or can't do. My goal for this book is to show you how you can practice mindfulness in the real world as an ordinary person without overwhelming yourself with too many rituals or actions. The best thing about mindfulness? It's free. It always has been and always will be.

Mindfulness & Awareness

To me, mindfulness and awareness are really important topics, and you may find certain parts of this book a bit repetitive. I hope you will forgive me. You see, I really want to make sure that I communicate well so that you understand my point well.

So how can mindfulness help you take your life to a whole new level? That phrase also sounds a bit over market-ish now that I think about it...

To make it simple - the more we practice mindfulness, the more aware we become. This is how we can make better decisions aimed at achieving a better life. We make better and healthier choices. Personally, I have noticed a massive improvement in my health and fitness thanks to mindfulness. Why? Because I was able to analyze negative patterns and habits. With mindfulness, I was able to embrace healthy mindful eating and healing. I found it very helpful to eradicate my emotional eating patterns. We will talk more about that later in this book.

Also, mindfulness helps us focus on where we're going, not where we're coming from. By taking a mindful approach, we learn from our mistakes. It's not about denying that bad things happened. Unfortunately, in this world, bad things can happen even to the most positive people. There is no guarantee for an eternally stress-free and problem-free life. But...mindfulness gives us tools to be proactive, not reactive.

Chapter 2 Transforming Your Life with Mindfulness

Mindfulness can also help you excel in your career. It helps you to dive deep to learn your strengths, what you're good at, and what you're not so good at. You will know what to focus on.

Mindfulness can even help you to gradually define your passions. For most people, including myself, it takes some time to get to know your passions, so don't worry if you are still trying to figure out what you're passionate about. You're not alone.

Besides, your passions and interests may always change. Mindfulness helps you become more aware of those shifts so that you can adapt and, if possible, change or re-adjust your professional path.

The same applies to relationships!

Mindfulness & Relationships

From my experience, most problems that people face in their relationships come from the following mistakes (and we have all been guilty of them):

-Not being able to communicate well.

-Not knowing what we really want.

-Expecting people to be perfect even though we are not.

-Not listening to other people, but demanding that they listen to us.

-Having either too much ego, or being too ashamed of oneself (both can be detrimental, I believe some levels of ego can be helpful for a healthy personal development, more on that later).

Mindfulness and Honesty

Honesty is lesson number 1. Before we really get into it, we must accept this Universal truth and become more humble. The truth is that we are asleep and the level of our mindfulness and awareness are low.

Even if we have been through programs on mindfulness, attended courses, and read books, we are still asleep, or almost asleep, and we still don't know it all. We might know enough to get started on living and practicing our mindful lifestyles, but again, we must accept the fact that we don't know it all and we will never know it all. There is no certification that will make us know it all or seem that we know it all.

This may be a hard pill to swallow, but I consider it to be a very important mantra. This mantra will teach us to be humble so that we can remain hungry. Hungry for what?

Awareness. Real awareness. Knowing ourselves.

Be hungry for awareness, put your ego down, and use this statement as a starting point.

Ego is a good thing in a mindful world. I believe that ego is great if it translates into passion, ambition, drive, and providing value to other people.

Ego can be detrimental if it makes us stop our quest by making us think that we know it all and there is nobody we can learn from. This can be very misleading for all of us, hence the mantra I mentioned earlier. This mantra will help us stay on the ground.

The truth is that our mind is always wandering. We can't stop what's on our mind, we can't have it blank. But we can be aware of what is going on and read through it to learn more about ourselves.

So this is good news if you have ever tried to meditate...

Maybe you got frustrated with meditation because you were not able to quieten your mind as much as you aimed for. No worries, you are not alone.

It's not possible to quieten your mind 100%, just like it's not possible to be 100% self-conscious. I think it is good news in a way. Nobody is perfect!

Also, remembering what was on our mind or what we saw does not always mean being self-conscious. We can remember all the details but still miss on the big picture.

Finally, we need to accept hard work, yes hard work, through mindfulness. It's like lifting some heavy weights to tone up your mindfulness muscles.

Reading this book alone will not help you become more mindful. You will need to take action and start practicing the techniques that I will show you and promise yourself you will not feel scared of self-honesty and diving deep.

You will do yourself a favor and look at yourself, your life, your actions, and thoughts from the outside. You will admit to yourself both the good and bad, exactly like it is. During this process, you may start feeling uncomfortable. There might be some shifts on your way. I am not saying this to be negative, I am saying this to help you prepare yourself for this journey.

The prize will be unleashing the power of mindfulness and awareness.

No shortcuts are needed. People often resort to drugs to achieve states of awareness, but instead of getting closer to those states, they are just getting further away from them.

Instead of getting rid of layers that prevent us from achieving a life full of happiness, drugs and other toxic substances only add to those layers and distractions.

What Kills Mindfulness?

There are also other things that kill mindfulness:

- Distractions - I'm referring to all kinds of addictions, even social media, shopaholism, and even some kinds of workaholism (I have been guilty of a few of those).

- Judgment - Here I'm referring to both positive and negative judgment. For example, some people are a bit naïve and believe in everything they see and hear. It's easy to manipulate them. These people will be the first ones to get manipulated by all kinds of advertisements and are very easy to be sold to. On the other hand, there are also people who are too negative, and they see dishonesty in all human beings. Both approaches lack mindfulness and what I call real personal investigation. They also very often reflect the relationships that people have had with themselves and what has happened to them in the past.

I would be dishonest to say I have never judged. Another mantra by Marta is: *We have all judged and we have all been judged, it's just how the world goes.*

I also believe that as long as we are alive, we will judge and be judged to some extent.

However, mindfulness can help us reduce the amount of judgment that very often results in suffering and unhappiness that we either get ourselves or create for other people.

Chapter 3 Mindfulness to Make Friends with Your Emotions and Enjoy Your Life Now

Mindless can mean "all the same." This can work out for some people, especially less sensitive people who feel good following the crowd. But if you are like me, and you have always felt a bit weird compared to your peers (I've had this feeling since I was a kid) and it means that you need to follow your own way. This is not to say that you and I are better than others. It's not about who is better or worse. It's about who decides to follow their truth of self-awareness. It's about who wants to feel re-awakened.

I know some people who are happy exactly where they are, doing what they are doing. I don't preach anything to them because I see them happy. Of course, if I were to live the way they live, I would not be happy, and I guess they would not be happy living their lives following my lifestyle. But again, it's not about who's right or wrong. It's about knowing yourself. Some people like to be asleep. Besides, all is subjective. I may think they are asleep, but they think they live their lives to the fullest. Again, who am I to judge those people?

Follow this definition - Mindful can mean different and unique. So don't worry if you have always had a feeling you were different. It's just the way you were meant to be. Maybe you have went through some pain, suffering, and rejection.

Maybe you cried thinking, "Why me? "Guess what, mindfulness can help you shift your perception. You can see your bad days, your pain, and your suffering as something that will provide inspiration to other people.

Be Hungry for Mindfulness

Every day, ask yourself for patience. This is what we all need. Patience is something that helps us enjoy our mindfulness cup of coffee even more!

Be grateful for who you are and accept yourself, but always look for that next level.

Mindfulness helps us embrace self-love, honest self -love, where there are also bad days. This is normal; we are not robots. We need those days to have a good and honest relationship with ourselves.

It's just like with a partner - you need to communicate well with each other. Now, think of yourself as your partner. Yes! Some people may judge you as egocentric, narcissistic, and who knows what else. Don't care about what others say.

For the time being, you only need to care about your mindfulness journey.

Put yourself first and take care of yourself so that you can transform yourself and take better care of those you love.

How to Actually Practice Mindfulness?

Even though you may not realize it, if you are reading this book carefully, just focusing on the current content and not getting too distracted thinking, "Why is this book so different compared to typical books on mindfulness?" You are already mindful.

Well, even if you do have such thoughts, this is absolutely normal. Perfection does not exist.

A spiritual guru would say that by being more mindful, we are less prone to judge, which is true. But a spiritual guru could also say that when we are mindless, we are quicker to judge, which is also true. However, by saying that, he is also kind of judging, right?

The way I see it is-just do the best you can, and whenever you get off track, get mindless and judgmental, and be aware of it. In other words, try to be mindful of your mindlessness, and try to be mindful of your dark side too.

In this day and age, we are very impatient. When it comes to books and information products... I recently invested in an online course related to marketing and entrepreneurship. To be honest, while going through the first lessons, I was thinking of returning it. I thought, "Man, this is just so basic!" Then I noticed that many people online were talking negatively about this course. I was actually disappointed in myself for buying it, and I was really on the verge of asking for refund. But then I wondered, how can I judge the course just by a few lessons? Why don't I give it a try and at least try to learn the rest of the material? Why do I trust other people's opinions? I haven't even studied all the lessons, and I have not applied them.

I therefore decided to re-watch the very first introductory lesson. While going through the course for the first time, I had skipped it, thinking that my time was too valuable to be wasted on the introduction. In this introduction, the creator of the course said just one thing. "Don't judge this course until you have watched all the lessons carefully." I decided to be mindful and had faith in the process. I realized that I was too biased and judgmental in my opinions. Subsequently, I watched the whole course and it gave me many brilliant ideas and strategies that I can now apply not only in my business, but to my life.

Other people missed it because they judged it just by the very few lessons they watched, and since it was different from the mainstream courses of this kind, they judged it too quickly. They were looking for this secret sauce that would make them successful. Then, instead of using their time carefully, they wasted it by going online and writing negative opinions about the course, even though they only did about 5 or 10% of it. They chose their own egos ("But I already know this stuff"!) and decided to stick to the same old, same old.

Of course, this is not about forcing yourself to like something you don't like or something that is not for you. Being mindful is not always super positive. It's about opening yourself up to learning and experience. It's about putting your ego down and being curious, like a kid.

Mindfulness will make you stronger so that you don't give up too early. And if you do give up, at least you will know that you tried your best.

I know people who come to yoga and they just give up after the very first lesson. They say: but I am not that flexible!

Can you see the *mindless pattern* here?

The best part is that they had already invested in fancy yoga mats and yoga pants only to say it was not for them!

Why? Most people are not mindful enough to realize that there is also a process and learning curve to everything. There is no reason to compare yourself to other people. For example, I could quit writing this book and say that I am not a good enough writer and English is my second language, or that I don't have the time to do it. And honestly, that is what the old Marta would say. However, the new Marta is more mindful now, and she knows the right dose of self-love and self-honesty. She knows how to trust her process and be mindful about it. Instead of focusing on problems, I focus on solutions. My super editor will heal this manuscript when needed and I am sure he will also have a few laughs at my English here and there!

Whatever it is that you need to do, there is always a learning curve. Even if you do something you are absolutely passionate about, there will always be certain mundane tasks that you will just have to do. This happens to me all the time. Again, mindfulness comes in very handy for me, both in my personal and professional life. Finally, thanks to mindfulness, you learn to be passionate about the process of whatever it is that you do.

I hope you got the general grasp of what mindfulness is and how it can be used in your everyday life. You can start being mindful right now. Don't give up thinking you are easily distracted or that it's not for you. By embracing mindfulness, you will have more quality of life and health, and you will be more successful in your career without overworking or overwhelming yourself.

The work I want you to do for the time being is very simple. Don't deviate from what I teach and do it every day. The simplicity of these exercises will make it easier for you to practice them every day, even when on holiday, and even when you're tired. Just give it a go! You can set up a daily alert on your mobile device to make sure you actually do these exercises.

Go for it and do them!

Mindfulness Exercises

The goal - Learn to perceive everything the way it is, both the good and the bad.

This is how you can be mindfully proactive and look for solutions.

Have the raw data of what's going on. By saying raw, I mean not through the lenses of your own emotions and meanings.

We will practice mindfulness through our senses and internal dialogues.

1. Sense: SEE

    Sit down, take a few deep breaths, and have a look at an object around you, preferably something static, like a table or cup. Look at it. Just notice it, that's it.

I am looking at my cup of green tea now. I embrace its yellow color. I keep breathing and looking at the cup. I really enjoy just staring at it.

By the way, if you are practicing this in an office or a room with other people, they will think you are going mad. I suggest you do it when you're on your own so that you can tune in better.

Keep focusing on the object. Notice all of the colors and patterns. Just keep seeing and don't judge. We don't care where the object is coming from, we don't care whether we like it or not. It's just there and we are observing it.

Good job, now it's time for the next step - our internal dialogue.
Register the fact that you are staring at the object.
That's the only thing you are doing.

Again, focus on eliminating your opinions. Just focus on the facts that your eyes are registering. Close your eyes and focus on the image again. In my case, it's a big yellow cup with grey elements, filled with green tea. I just try to focus on the colors and shape, not on what I should do with the cup or where's it coming from.

It is the way it is and that's the way I register it.

Remember, this mindfulness exercise is just about savoring, and just about enjoying.

2. Hearing

Focus on what you can hear around you. Take a few deep breaths and focus.

In this day and age, we very often hear, but we don't truly listen. We are not mindful and not tuned in enough.

For now, just for a few minutes, all we need to do is to focus on what we can hear.

In my case, it is birds singing, some cars passing by, and my own breath. I don't give it any meaning.

What about you. What can you hear?

Now focus on your internal dialogue. Label it as it is. Note it as it is within reality.

3. Feeling

You can do this exercise either standing up or sitting down.

It's up to you. Since I have been at my desk for quite a few hours now, I will stand up just to wake up a bit.

If standing up, all you need to do is stand up and be comfortable. Focus on the sensation between your feet and the floor.

If sitting down, all you need to do is to feel your butt (I know it sounds weird) or your feet touching the ground.

Now go inside and label it as it is. Without overcomplicating it. It doesn't matter how you judge it. Just focus on the essence. The raw essence. No cooking and no seasoning. Notice it the way it is. Keep breathing and noticing.

******

I hope you enjoyed this simple exercise. However, the best part is yet to come!

Unfortunately, this part is the most difficult and challenging for most of us. Luckily, this is what can result in optimal change that can shift us in the right direction - the direction we need to be in!

You see, in the previous exercise, we focused on outer sensations. But now it's time to dive deep and focus on inner sensations. This is what it's really all about, and this is where most people quit. Of course, I don't want you to quit, so bear with me. And even if you quit, don't judge yourself and the fact that you quit, because you can always re-commit and go back to it later. I quit many things many times in the past, but thanks to mindfulness, I was able to re-evaluate why I quit, and in many cases I decided to get back to certain activities and goals feeling stronger and more empowered.

OK, so let's do it! Have no fear!

Inner Mindfulness - How to Make GOOD Friends with Your Emotions

First of all, emotions are feedback. Yes, both good and bad emotions are feedback.

There is no reason for blocking out emotions and pretending it's OK. In this day and age of over-political correctness, where we all should appear as happy, proper, and just perfect, many of us tend to block our emotions.

I think this is a problem. I used to do it myself until one morning back in 2012. That morning, I just couldn't get out of bed. At that time, I was "OK," or I thought I was. I had a corporate job and was living for the weekends. Of course, there is nothing wrong with having a job if you enjoy it, or at least it does not affect your health in a negative way. So yeah, I thought I was OK, and I kept telling myself that it was OK because I was doing what everyone else around me was doing. Until one morning I just suddenly felt paralyzed. I thought, "What's happening, how is this possible? I am supposed to be a positive person. It's OK, I will be OK." But it wasn't OK. So I had to two choices: go and see a doctor and ask for some magic pills to be OK, or mindfully embrace the fact that it wasn't OK. Many of my friends back home thought that my life in a big city, abroad, in a sunny country was the ultimate dream, and so was a corporate job in multilingual customer service, obviously it was not for me. I was working myself towards sickness and exhaustion and I felt lost. At that time, I decided to be honest with myself. The first step was to honestly label how I felt without judging or correcting it.

And I knew I felt unfulfilled, emotionally drained, and disappointed with myself.

I realized I wasn't achieving my goals, but someone else's goals.

At that time, I could have gone on sick leave like many of my colleagues were doing, but I knew it would make things worse. So I just called my boss and apologized. I said that I overslept and I turned up to work a bit late, but man! I was changed.

At least I knew that what I was doing as far as my job was concerned was temporary. At least I knew I had to embrace self-care, mindfulness, and holistic personal development.

Some would say – oh, just quit your job! And yes, in many cases I agree. I evolved from an employee to an entrepreneur. However, we also need to be mindful about it. Most people can't afford to quit their jobs from one day to another, and usually it's not very smart or well thought out. I had done it before as well, only to end up looking for another job 2 or 3 months later.

This is why by embracing self-honesty, self-truth, and mindfulness, my mantra was, "This is not what I want to do for the rest of my life. But I am grateful for this position for the time being because it pays my bills and it will help me transition to a better career."

Now, this journey is a topic for another book and not really relevant now.

But mindfulness was my biggest remedy at that time.

I began researching and learning about meditation. At that time, as a fast-paced city girl, I thought meditation was a bit pointless, so it was a massive shift for me. Most guided meditations would not work for me, so I decided to create my own, simple one... Marta's Mindfulness Meditation. I would just sit down and focus on all my senses. Sometimes with no logical order, just letting it go. Then I would do my inner mindfulness meditation and my inner scan, asking myself about how I felt. Then I would also journal without hiding anything from myself.

To sum up:

- Emotions are feedback. View them as colors, feel them as sensations, they just are.

Don't just hear them, actually *listen* to them. They are trying to guide you in a mindful way.

- All changes on your journey to mindfulness are a process. While retreats and seminars are great, you won't achieve your ultimate mindfulness mastery by paying a guru X for his latest product or workshop. You will need to do your own part and dive deep.

- It's absolutely normal to have weaker periods of time where you just feel a bit more negative, irritable or sad. Even the most positive people have those periods of time. While I am not a professional therapist or counselor, and I am not offering any specific advice for depressive or anxious states, I can only share my experience and the process that works for me. I simply slow down, tune in, and spend more time in meditation. I also try to be honest with myself and ask myself what I can do to move forward with the flow and how to make changes in my life in a mindful way.

- We can't always control what happens to us, but we can choose to be mindful about it. However, mindful will not always mean "but I am OK" even if you are not OK. Mindful means 'as it is now,' so don't be scared of giving yourself honest answers that will allow you make mindful decisions so that you can achieve real peace and happiness.

Chapter 4 Transform All Areas of Your Life and Health with Mindful Self-Honesty

Many of my subscribers reply to my newsletters saying that they either feel a deep sense of relief or sometimes they are just slightly surprised with my simple approach to mindfulness and life. While some, of course, may find my honesty and directness too overwhelming for them or are just not ready for it yet, many state that just by realizing that sometimes it's OK *not* to be OK, they realized that they no longer had to waste their energy masking the problem, but can actually use it to mindfully explore it.

In my *Holistic Mindfulness Newsletters,* I share the good and the bad about my journey. I have also noticed that many people get slightly surprised that I don't just write things like, "Hey, life is good, and it's always so beautiful and amazing because we are all mindful." I think that if someone has a bad day or there is something unpleasant going on in their lives, they may actually get pissed off when they receive a fluffy, over-feel good stuff like that. But I actually give simple strategies like in this book and underline one fact: *negative emotions are just feedback.*

Let me give you this example; it's the only one that comes to my mind now. Now, I am not a mom, so I am not giving any advice on parenting. It's just an example to illustrate my point:

Imagine a mom or dad with a small kid. The kid is crying, screaming, and pointing to their belly. What would most parents do? Well, most parents, assuming they are in their right senses, would assume that their kid is sick, probably suffering from food poisoning or maybe a bacteria, and would act quickly by taking their child to a doctor to see what the problem was and find a cure.

They would not just say to the kid, "Just smile, you are OK. Your belly is fine. Just be happy, and it will be fine. Just love yourself. Breathe in and out. You should be fine now!"

I hope you get my point. It's mastering inner mindfulness that is the most difficult part. That is why from now on, I want you to do this exercise every day:

Again we will focus on:

1. Seeing
2. Hearing
3. And feeling

But this time, we will scan our emotions and what's inside.

I want you to sit still and focus on breathing in and out.

Just relax for a few minutes. Breathe in and out. Breathe in: mindful, awakening energy.

Breathe out mindless illusions...

Now, this part will be simple and natural for us. Why? Well, it would be hard if I told you to 'just mediate and eliminate all of your thoughts.' Why? Because it's hard to eliminate all of your thoughts. In fact it's not possible at all!

So what we will be doing in this mindfulness meditation is simply scanning and label our thoughts and emotions.

Let's say the first thought that comes to your mind is that you have to do something.

OK, that's fine!

"I have to write this report. I have to write this report."

Now here's the trick. Our mindless mind, also called "monkey mind," will try to come up with all possible scenarios to make us anxious. For example - "I won't have enough time, I will mess up, other colleagues will do it better, I will not get this promotion," and similar.

Here's what you need to do. Get back to the main thought and just stay with it, just like it is.

I have to write this report.

See it, hear it, and feel it. Label it as it is without seeing it too negatively or over-positively. Just see it as it is.

I have to write this report.

When you're ready, focus on the next thought or feeling.

Sometimes it may even be something like:

My belly is digesting my lunch. My belly is digesting my lunch.

I feel grateful. I feel satisfied.

There no real set way to do it. I believe that everyone does it in their own way.

The reason why I write books on mindfulness and what I call holistic self-help is simply to let you know my way. I believe that when trying things out, you will figure out your own process that works for you. My suggestions are merely a starting point on your journey. As I always underline, I am not a spiritual guru, and it is not my intention to become one.

I am your friend, and we are on this journey together.

Practicing Mindfulness in Everyday Situations

What if you don't have time to sit and meditate all day long? Well, this is something I talk about in my other book on mindfulness called "Mindfulness for Busy People" (published in May 2015).

It all starts off with you making a decision to make mindfulness your lifestyle. For example, you can choose to be mindful while commuting to work. Or you can choose to be mindful while doing your dishes.

You can even choose to be mindful when doing certain tasks you don't really enjoy. With mindfulness, you can learn to be passionate about whatever it is that you do. Anything that you know will help you grow personally, spiritually, or professionally.

In this day and age, we are very picky and choosey, and we only what to do the things we love and are passionate about. While I believe that in long term, it makes sense to create your professional path around something you are passionate about. I also recognize the fact that sometimes in order to follow our passions, we must go through certain processes and tasks that we are not really that passionate about. There is a learning curve to everything. This is where many people give up and say 'but I don't enjoy it,' or 'but this is not my passion.'

However, taking a mindful approach and putting the ego down, we may ask ourselves: will doing this task help me live my passion long-term?

Also, the line "just follow your passion" sounds great, but really, if it was so easy, everyone would be happy with their jobs. They would just follow their passions and get paid for it straight away. In this scenario, nobody would ever complain about their jobs or businesses.

However, reality is different. I can honestly tell you that I enjoy what I do, and I do follow my passion. I also believe that mindfully listening to one's gut and asking oneself, "What is my purpose, and how can I provide value?" helps.

But I can also honestly tell you that in order to be able to follow my passion and do what I love, there were many tasks and processes I had to go through, and I wasn't always that passionate about them. I just learned to take a mindful approach and moved forward.

Even now, there are many aspects of my business that I am not passionate about, and even though now I have a team, there are still certain tasks I have to do myself and can't delegate them. I am not always passionate about them, but I know they allow me to focus on the bigger picture and live my passion long-term. In real life, there is always some sacrifice, sweat, and tears. And again, I don't mean to be negative, and not everything we do has to be achieved the hard way. We also need to be open to receiving. But the best use of mindfulness is knowing and accepting your reality first, being honest with yourself, and then trying to look for something good in bad, learning to be peaceful, mindful, and patient, and moving forward. Don't get discouraged from achieving your dreams. You now have mindfulness in your holistic toolbox of self-development!

Don't allow your mind to get lost in negative stories. Look at things holistically, as they are, but always cultivate gratitude and try to be mindfully passionate about the process of transforming your life with every single step you take.

Maybe you want to lose weight or increase your energy levels. The mindful approach could be this: every day, start journaling and stating how you feel and what you want. Then write your long-term vision for how you want your body to be.

Then, focus on the here and now. Write down 3 simple actions that you can take today that will bring you closer to your goal. Just 3, and no more. This could be having a nice salad for lunch, going for a walk or run, or signing up for some healthy cooking classes that you could attend in the evenings and on the weekend. Don't get too carried away. In the evening, journal again expressing gratitude for the fact that you completed your mini goals. This will give you energy and motivation to carry on this process the next day, and then again the next day.

It will make your life easier and will help you transform your mindset so that you can mindfully achieve your goals.

Mindfulness and Honest Self-Love

How to embrace self-love in an honest and mindful way?

Well, let's have a look at this story...

There are two friends, let's call them Ann and Jane. Both are not very happy with their lives, but they pretend it's OK, and if necessary, they fix themselves with medical drugs or go on shopping sprees. They are both overweight and know that they need to change their relationship with food. Neither of them likes their job. They both feel lonely, but never try to meet new people.

Their life continues the same day after day, and they would both like to change something, but still feel stuck to the same old same old. In the evening, they usually go shopping together, buying things that they don't need to impress people they don't even care about.

Sometimes they get drunk with friends, or order fast food and sit on the couch watching TV.

Now, one of the two friends, Ann, decides to change her life. First, she starts attending seminars during the weekends and learns how to work on her motivation and mindset to change things in her life. During those seminars, she meets like-minded people and starts hanging out with them. They all have similar goals. Because of that, she is not able to hang out with Jane as much as she used to, but she still wants to have her as a friend and cares about her. This is why she keeps telling her about upcoming workshops, seminars, or even invites her to lunch with her new friends.

Jane never accepts those invitations. She prefers to stick to her old ways. She believes that Ann is too into herself and doesn't care about her old friends. She feels talked down to even though Ann does not judge her and simply wants to help her meet new people.

Finally, a few months pass by. During those few months, Ann feels empowered to change her nutrition, go to the gym, and lose weight. She transforms her body and becomes really passionate about health and fitness. She decides to carry on her path and become a health coach.

Now she wants to have a passion-based business where she can help other people transform their bodies, embrace self-love, eat healthier, etc.

Of course, such an ambitious goal takes some time to accomplish, and on her journey to starting her own business, there are many ups and downs and a bit of a learning curve as well. But finally, she is transformed, becomes very popular amongst her clients, and is able to quit her job and start her own business.

Jane doesn't like it. She feels attacked. Instead of being happy about her best friend's success, she begins avoiding her and talks behind her back. "Ann is so into herself! She is so stupid. She quit her job, I bet she will be back begging for it. She can't make a decent living from her business! She thinks she is better than others because she lost weight. I bet she is anorexic now and doesn't eat at all, what kind of a life is that?" or:

"She doesn't attend any of the parties we used to go to because she is always busy with her certifications, trainings, and who knows what. I bet it's all a scam and she is giving her money to some charlatans who won't teach her anything. She will be sorry!"

Jane sees a few friends, and they talk about Ann's success and transformation. Other friends' advice to Jane is:

"Don't worry Jane, just love yourself!"

So Jane takes this advice and lives the same way she used to live, but the problem is that her lifestyle is making her even more sick, tired, and depressed.

Now, is this an example of real self-love? Or is it an example of just pretending it's all OK?

Is Jane's lifestyle helping her be happy, or is it just an escape from a reality she doesn't like?

Finally, who is really practicing self-love in an honest, mindful way? Jane or Ann?

Now don't get me wrong, not everyone needs to drastically change their lives like Ann did. If you are happy where you are and it's not damaging your physical and emotional health, it's fine.

But speaking of mindfulness, we need to be honest about what we think and do.

This story shows that what was really happening is that Jane had too much ego to admit she was getting scared of her friend's success and effort.

Instead of admitting to herself where the real emotions were coming from, she felt better accusing her friend of too much ego and not accepting her help.

Jane's definition of self-love was "I will stay where I am" instead of "I will mindfully scan my situation and try to take some positive actions so that I can enjoy better health. I know that if I carry on drinking, doing drugs and eating fast food, I could develop serious health issues, even cancer, and I love myself enough to put my ego down and ask for help because I deserve to learn how to live healthier."

What do you think?

Mindfulness for Ordinary People

Some days will be better, and some days will be worse. Again, this is nothing but your own judgment. Also, remember that practicing mindfulness does not mean that all your problems will magically evaporate and you will start levitating and seeing auras in 7 days or less.

There is a lot of hype out there. The inner mindfulness practice is really working on your mindfulness muscle. The most important thing is to just go ahead and do it. Put your ego down and have faith in the process.

Now, since I have used the phrase, "Just put your ego down," I would like to stop and talk about that too. Why? Well, because I see that there are quite a few misconceptions regarding this phrase, and many of them can be detrimental to our holistic personal development.

Is ego always bad?

Most spiritual books say that ego is bad for our holistic self-growth, and I definitely don't disagree. But I also believe that there is a positive side to ego that, when embraced, can be very beneficial. As always, it's all about mindful balance.

Ego is good if it translates into passion, ambition, flexibility in your approach, drive, and the desire to provide value. Whether you want to provide value to your family and community through your everyday life, provide value to your clients through your work, or provide value to the company or organization you are working for and help them grow. Ego is good if it appears as a hunger for knowledge and growth. Ego is good if it pushes us to expand, stretch, and grow.

At the same time, ego can be destructive if it results in greed, jealousy, and judgment. It's destructive if a person is not flexible and wants to blindly achieve their goals without caring whether or not they will hurt other people in the process. A person with too much ego, even if they're passionate about what they do, is less likely to succeed because they will always focus more on themselves and what they want instead of on what their clients want. The same applies to their personal life. A person with too much ego will find it hard to build up long-lasting and happy relationships.

Too much ego can prevent us from listening. But a mindful person will know how to smartly and mindfully use their ego to result in positive ambition and drive to move forward. This is why a mindful person won't be too scared to reach out for help and ask someone who is more successful for their guidance.

A mindless and egoistic person won't ask for help, thinking they know it all.

They will reject even the best coaches and mentors as charlatans or "total beginners."

They will focus too much on their past achievements and how great they are and will refuse to go on the part of holistic personal development.

How do I know?

I used to be that mindless, egoistical person.

Chapter 5 Mindfulness for Deep Transformation and Long-Lasting Change

It wasn't until I reached the bottom and all areas of my life crashed that I decided to do something about it. Mindfulness was one of the first things I found, and I learned to use my ego in a positive way. I used it to set certain goals for myself to evolve in the right direction.

Mindfulness and Overprotecting Others

Even though I have been practicing mindfulness for a few years now, this is what I recently discovered after doing some deep soul diving. There is always something to learn, and the reason why I am so open about my experiences and imperfections is so that you have some real-life references and examples.

The drive to help others and give them the proper tools to help them on their journey (whether it's health, life, relationships, or career) is a beautiful thing. Don't get me wrong.

However, I have learned that everyone has their own process, and in order to grow and learn, they will, and probably even should, make their own mistakes.

To put it simply, help others when they need it. But don't overdo it because they might think that you don't believe in them or that you think you are better than they are.

I used to lecture people about health all the time, even when they were not interested in listening to me.

Now I take a mindful approach, and instead of just lecturing like "do this, eat this don't eat that thing," I say, "I have been through this journey, and I can always share my experience with you. If you want, or if you are ready, let me know.

Most people hate being lectured unless they ask for a lecture. Even though you are trying to help, they may see it as a personal attack.

Of course, if I see that someone has a serious problem, I will share whatever information I have that can help them solve it, but with mindfulness. I do it in a friendly and non-judgmental way.

Mindfulness and Journaling

If you are ready for the next step, I suggest you go through this journaling exercise.

You can either do it in regards to your life in general, or in a specific area of your life. Then you can repeat the same process to analyze other areas of your life.

Divide a piece of paper into 3 parts.

The first part is called: *What I really mindfully want*

The second part is called: *What I need to mindfully start doing to get there*

The third part: *What I need to mindfully give up to get there*

Unfortunately, the third part is what most people don't like, and I don't blame them. But again, sometimes it's not about what you like or what you don't like. It's just the way it is.

We must accept the good and the bad.

The next step is to take action. But I am not referring just "taking massive action" the guru way.

I am referring to taking meaningful and purposeful action in the right direction to avoid unnecessary stress. And if stress happens again, you will mindfully scan yourself to get to the root of the problem and deal with it in a holistic way. What is causing you the stress?

This is what true self-love is all about. It's not about saying it's OK when it's not OK. It's not about saying "but I just love myself." It's about mindful self-honesty.

Let's say a person does the above-mentioned exercise to improve their health and fitness.

What I really mindfully want

I want a slim body, to be healthy, and have tons of energy.

What mindful actions will I take?

Eat more fruits and vegetables. Learn healthy recipes so that I can still eat ice cream and pizza, but in their healthier, possibly plant-based versions. Move my body more. Join the gym. Be out on my bike more.

What will I mindfully give up?

Eating fast food. Sitting on my couch watching TV. Spending too much time glued to my mobile device when I could go for a walk and listen to a motivational audiobook instead.

OK, so the person is now mindfully revising this plan every day.

Now there are 2 extreme scenarios that can happen. Both can be detrimental and certainly lack mindfulness:

First - the person overdoes everything, such as doing extreme starvation diets and over-exercising to "lose weight fast," and they either get tired and give up to go back to the same old same old, or they get some health issues because everything in overdose is not good for us. I think that makes sense.

Second - the person looks at the plan and rebels against it straight away.

"But I love myself! I deserve my fast food and burgers and ice cream. Who are you to tell me what to do? You are slim because you are lucky, or maybe you are just starving yourself. Healthy eating is boring. I just love myself, and I love my choices, so I am not changing anything." So what can happen is that this person will only put on more weight and eventually can develop some serious health issues. Possibly even cancer.

Both scenarios are bad and totally lack mindfulness.

A mindful person, with the right dose of self-love, is proactive and looks at things as they are in an honest way. They are patient and trust the process. They use their ego to remind themselves of their goals, but put it down to reach out for help and admit that they don't know it all. They will use failure to learn and progress. They will use negative emotions as their feedback to guide them. They will look at more successful people not as objects of hate, but as mentors and inspiration to give them strength to move forward in their journey.

They will not falsely and mindlessly use the very often over-hyped concept of self-love to give up on their dreams before they have even started.

They will mindfully use the healthy dose of self-humor and embrace their imperfections, gradually moving forward, following their own pace.

They will mindfully notice and reward their efforts and celebrate every little success and even every little failure because it is also a step towards success.

This is what I call real, strong, unconditional mindful self-love. I hope this book is providing you with ideas as for how to embrace it.

Mindfulness and Criticizing Others

This was a massive shift for me and making this shift has helped me drastically improve all areas of my health, life, and career.

I used to be very fond of criticizing others and looking at their faults. Until, after diving deep and going through this mindful path of self-development, I realized that I was mostly criticizing myself and my own insecurities.

This was a big truth for me, and I am still on my journey to implementing it as much as I can.

Mindfulness for Anxiety

It usually happens that we focus on what we don't have instead of what we do have.

With mindfulness, we can look at the situation from a different perspective. For example, you may think you don't have or own enough, but for someone else, your life may be the ultimate dream.

There are many countries where people cannot afford to or cannot access methods to order this book. For many of us is it may just be a cheap eBook or a short little book, but for someone else, the cost may be someone's food for a day or even two days. Mindfulness encourages us to think about this planet and its people.

It's not only about us. Thanks to taking this approach and looking at our own problems from a different perspective, we may actually realize that we don't really have so many problems to begin with.

Mindfulness for Laziness

I believe that there are 2 kinds of laziness, and thanks to the process of mindfulness and mindful scans, both can be cured.

The first one is when a person is simply burned out after going through an intense workaholic grind phase. I have been guilty of this, I admit it.

The problem here is not really laziness, even though it may seem that way at first. The problem may be that the person is either physically or mentally tired, or has already achieved their materialistic goals.

In both scenarios, mindfulness can help find two simple solutions. First of all, slow down. Your body and mind need it. Relax so that you can be active and productive again. As a second solution in case a person has lost their motivation, they may want to re-evaluate their goals and shift more to contribution or something that is bigger than them. This will work for people who worked hard to achieve something like a certain amount of money per month, a new car, or a house, and now they have a nice lifestyle but feel like they have lost their drive and passion.

What can help is mindful goal-setting and making your goals super exciting.

Sometimes you also need to ask yourself: Do you need to slow down or take more action?

Sometimes you need to do the opposite of what you think. It's as simple as that.

Now, the second scenario is when a person gets a bit overwhelmed and doesn't know where to start, or maybe they have faced lots of pain and rejection. For example, imagine someone who lost their job and now they are at their parents' house, trying to find a new job and being judged for "being lazy."

Well, what is really happening here is that the person is anxious or depressed. Some people are more sensitive and find it harder to adapt to change. If you are one of those people, accept it and focus on the root of the problem. Embrace mindfulness to stay focused and centered. Don't take on more than what you can. Be sure you journal and start your day with simple and doable actions that will help you move forward. Avoid super-long to-do lists as they will only keep you paralyzed.

Mindfulness and Shiny Object Syndrome

Whatever it is that you are planning to do, whether it's committing to a new healthy eating plan or starting a new business, be sure you commit to one thing mindfully until you get some sort of results that will help you determine whether the given process works for you or not.

You have probably heard about people who go on a different diet every week and buy books on different diets but never actually read them fully.

It's the same with business. I have seen people jumping from one venture to another because they have seen someone making X amount of money with a different business and now they think they should do it too.

However, it's all about focus. Mindful focus. Our attention and concentration span are limited. You can't do it all at once. You may see someone successful with a certain diet program or a certain kind of business, and it may seem like an easy, overnight success. But did you have the chance to see the backstage and all the energy they put into the process? It requires incredible amounts of mindful energy and focus. It's as simple as that.

Mindfulness to Let Go and Achieve Peace

It's not about avoiding negative feelings and escaping from them, but it's also not about dwelling on them.

You know those voices in your head commenting on certain unpleasant situations? Maybe someone was rude to you or you feel that you said something stupid?

You probably know the solution: Just stop indulging in the same inner conversation every 20 minutes.

But the question is: how do you do it? Here's where mindfulness comes handy.

Instead of focusing on what happened and feeling bad about it, it's better to breathe in and out.

Scan your negative feeling from the inside out. You can give it a color and visualize it going away.

At the same time, don't bury it and don't deny it. All of those feeling are feedback.

Mindfulness and Gratitude

Here are my mindful gratitude rules:

Practice gratitude every day, not just on Thanksgiving.

Celebrate life every day, not just on your birthday.

Tell others how much you love them not only during family occasions.

Find joy in giving and receiving all year long.

Don't beat yourself up.

Focus on progress and be grateful for your own pace.

Whenever you're facing failure and adversity, mindfully scan the situation.

State the facts and look for solutions.

Finally, remember...

"When walking, walk. When eating, eat."- Zen proverb

Conclusion

Whatever it is that you are doing is a gift. Why? Because your time here is the most precious asset you were given.

Use this time to mindfully love, breathe, and feel alive. Try to inspire others even if you have a bad day. Many people will resonate with the fact that you tell them that you are not feeling confident or happy. While people don't like constant complainers, it's normal for even the happiest and most mindful people to have a bad day. This is what I call an approach that is both positive and realistic. We all need to dive deep, be more loving, compassionate, and help one another. I believe that mindfulness is an incredible tool, and we can all unleash its power. Keep practicing mindfulness your own way and do what feels right for you.

Finally, since I am always looking for honest feedback, I would love to hear from you in the review section of this book.

I would like to know what you think about this book, what you felt while reading it, how you think it can help you, and whether it was able to inspire you on your journey.

It's you I am writing for, and your opinion is of paramount importance for me. I take all kinds of feedback.

So go ahead and write a short review. It will only take a few seconds of your time, and it can also help other readers get interested in mindfulness so that they can receive its amazing benefits. Thanks in advance, I would love to hear from you!

For more inspiration visit:

www.holisticwellnessproject.com

Let's connect:

www.facebook.com/HolisticWellnessProject

www.instagram.com/Marta_Wellness

Contact:

info@holisticwellnessproject.com

Free Gifts from Marta

Free Audiobook: Mindfulness for Busy People

Download Link:

www.holisticwellnessproject.com/mindfulness

Free Audiobook: Guided Meditation

Download Link:

www.holisticwellnessproject.com/subscribe-newsletter

Free eBook: Holistically Productive

Download link:

www.holisticwellnessproject.com/subscribe-newsletter

86680127R00040

Made in the USA
Lexington, KY
14 April 2018